A COMPLIMENTARY REVIEW COPY, FALL 1969 OCT 1970

A WORLD EXPLORER BOOK

A World Explorer: Fridtjof Nansen

BY ERICK BERRY

ILLUSTRATED BY WILLIAM HUTCHINSON

ABOUT THE BOOK: This story of the life of Fridtjof Nansen is the fascinating biography of an author, scientist, and statesman as well as the exciting adventure story of a daring Norwegian explorer. Nansen's several expeditions took him deep into the icy unexplored region of the North Pole, where he and his companions often traveled with only dog-drawn sledges and kayaks. This book is part of Garrard's WORLD EXPLORER series, which offers young readers fast-moving adventure-filled biographies of the world's most famous explorers. Historically accurate, these books make ideal enrichment reading.

Subject classification: Social Studies, Biography
Sub-classification: North Pole Exploration, Reading, Information

ABOUT THE AUTHOR: Erick Berry's first work with children's books was as an illustrator. She then turned to editorial work and has edited a number of series for various publishers and has herself written numerous books. She and her husband, Herbert Best, have lived in many places and have written about most of them, including Nigeria; northern New York; New York City; Devon, England; Connecticut; the Philadelphia area, and Jamaica, West Indies. She is also the author of Garrard's *Leif the Lucky* and *Robert E. Peary* as well as *When Wagon Trains Rolled to Santa Fe*.

Reading Level: Grade 4   Interest Level: Grades 3–6
96 pages . . . 6½ x 9   Publisher's Price: $2.59
SBN 8116-6465-1

Illustrated in color; full-color jacket; reinforced binding

GARRARD PUBLISHING COMPANY

7. The Fram hit open water here.

THE ASTROLABE, an instrument developed by the Greeks, is the symbol for World Explorer Books. At the time of Columbus, sailors used the astrolabe to chart a ship's course. The arm across the circle could be moved to line up with the sun or a star. Using the number indicated by the pointer, a sailor could tell his approximate location on the sea. Although the astrolabe was not completely accurate, it helped many early explorers in their efforts to conquer the unknown.

World Explorer Books are written especially for children who love adventure and exploration into the unknown. Designed for young readers, each book has been tested by the Dale-Chall readability formula. Leo Fay, Ph.D., Professor of Education at Indiana University, is educational consultant for the series. Dr. Fay, an experienced teacher and lecturer, is well known for his professional bulletins and text material in both elementary reading and social studies.

A WORLD EXPLORER

Fridtjof Nansen

BY ERICK BERRY

ILLUSTRATED BY WILLIAM HUTCHINSON

GARRARD PUBLISHING COMPANY
CHAMPAIGN, ILLINOIS

For Ane Ingeborg Marguerite Skiderness Street,
my favorite Nordski, with love

This series is edited by Elizabeth Minot Graves

Contents

1
A Surprise Present

One snowy afternoon in Norway, in the year 1870, nine-year-old Fridtjof Nansen sat reading in his room. He was so deep in his book that he hardly heard the sleigh bells jingling outside. The sleighs were coming along the road from the city of Christiania, today called Oslo. They were bringing skiers to Huseby Hill, a mile beyond the Nansen farm.

"Fridtjof," said his mother, bending over him, "your sister has been calling you. Why don't you go and see what she wants?"

"A package has come for you," called his sister.

Fridtjof ran downstairs to see what it was. This was not yet Christmas. Who would be sending him a present?

Fridtjof's brother Alexander, only a year younger, eyed the long thin package curiously. "Open it! Open it!" he cried. "It looks like skis!"

All the family loved to ski, even Mother. Fridtjof had been skiing since he was four years old. But he owned only an old pair of skis, patched and hard to use.

Eagerly he untied the package. There, indeed, was a beautiful pair of shiny red skis, each with a black stripe painted down the middle.

"Oh, they're beautiful!" Fridtjof cried.

"They're from Father's friend, Mr. Fabritius," Mother said. "He knew how much you longed for a new pair."

With the skis was an eight-foot pole. In Norway in those days, only one long ski pole was used.

Fridtjof slung the skis over his shoulder and opened the front door. He simply must try them right away.

"Put on your coat," called Mother. But Fridtjof did not stop. It was very cold out, but he never minded the cold. He often went without coat or hat, even in bitter weather.

The beautiful new skis were far too fine to use on the little hill behind the farmhouse. He plunged off through the snow towards Huseby Hill.

First he tried the skis on the lower slope. They were even faster than he had imagined, and they moved easily as he swung to a stop. Two other skiers flashed by on their way down from the hilltop.

Fridtjof felt he must try his new skis from the top. He started upward, passing the ski jump. It was too bad that his puppy, Storm, wasn't along, but dogs were not allowed on the ski hill. Neither were small boys.

At the top he waited a moment, looking down the long shining slope ahead of him, then he pushed off. The snow was deep, but the trail had been well packed by other skiers. His heart pounded with excitement as he went faster and faster.

The ski jump rose ahead, a high platform of snow. It was much bigger than the jump on the hill behind his home. Suddenly he was at the end of the platform. His skis left the ground, and he

was flying through space like an eagle.

Only a few seconds passed, but it seemed much longer. Then he hit the ground.

Fridtjof made a bad landing. The tips of his skis caught in the snow and he was thrown straight into a snowbank. He could not breathe, but someone started to pull at his heels. Two men, who set him on his feet, were laughing in a friendly way. One of them handed him his skis which were not harmed at all.

The men brushed him down. "Those are beautiful skis," one said. They were indeed beautiful. For a happy moment Fridtjof had felt as if he had wings.

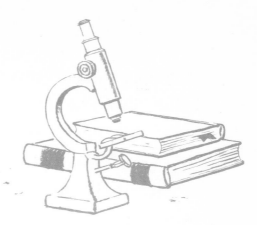

2

Nordmarka Forest

Fridtjof Nansen loved life on the big
farm, Store Fröen. He and Alexander
and their older brothers helped care for
the sheep and cattle and geese. Every
day the boys walked to their school, two
miles away in Christiania, Norway's cap-
ital. There Fridtjof's father went every
day to his law office.

Nansen was popular at school. He was

a good student and a fine athlete. He often brought his friends home to the farm. In winter they skated on the river that ran beside the house, or skied on Huseby Hill. In summer they swam and fished, and they could sail on Christiania fjord, a long arm of the sea, nearby.

Most of all Fridtjof enjoyed the wild Nordmarka forest, north of the farm. By the time he was twelve, Fridtjof had explored this wonderful wilderness whenever he could. Here was all a boy could wish for. Enormous trees arched over the many swift streams filled with fish. There were lakes to swim in and game to hunt.

In May, as soon as the trout were jumping, Fridtjof and Alexander gulped down an early breakfast and were off for a weekend of fishing. They headed straight for the Nordmarka River.

The summer daylight lasts twenty hours in Norway. Near midnight, weary and content, the boys would crawl into bed in a deserted hut. They would sleep for two or three hours and would then awake to start fishing again.

By the time he was fourteen, Fridtjof often went off alone to fish, hunt, or ski. When he caught fish or game he grilled it over a fire. If he caught nothing he was content to go without food. He slept on the bare ground.

Fridtjof was interested in everything he saw in the forest—rocks, trees, and animals. He always wanted to know more about them.

He was also interested in science. He and a friend tried chemistry experiments in the family attic. Fridtjof liked carpentry and was skillful with tools.

Nansen was tall for his age and had fair hair, blue eyes, and a warm smile. His outdoor life helped to make him unusually strong. When he was eighteen he broke the world's skating record for the mile. Over the years, he won the Norwegian championship twelve times for cross-country skiing.

Fridtjof graduated from high school with high honors and entered the University of Christiania. This university had been founded some 60 years before by his great-uncle, Count Herman von Wedel-Jarlsberg. Fridtjof continued to live at home and to walk into Christiania every day. He wanted to be close to the forests and the hills.

During his years in college Nansen was puzzled about his future career. He drew and painted well. Perhaps he could be an artist. Mathematics also interested him, as did science. Nansen spoke several languages and liked poetry. Perhaps he should be a writer. At last, with the advice of Robert Collett, a professor at the university, he decided to specialize in science, particularly zoology. This would combine his love of research with his love of outdoor life. There was a great deal of research to be done on both land and sea animals.

One morning, soon after Nansen had graduated from college, Professor Collett sent for him. "A seal-hunting ship, the *Viking*, leaves soon for the North," Professor Collett said. "I have told the captain that you are a good shot. He has offered to take you on as one of his crew. This would be a fine chance to study arctic animal life."

It would mean several months of research as well as of adventure. Nansen did not hesitate to accept.

"You can make a study of the ocean currents," the professor continued. "The college will lend you instruments to record winds and water temperature."

And so began the first of Nansen's famous expeditions to the North.

3

The *Viking* Sails North

Twenty-year-old Nansen was aboard the seal-hunting ship, *Viking*, when she sailed on March 11, 1882. The sea was rough and Nansen was seasick. Still, he kept careful notes of the speed and direction in which the ocean currents flowed. Certain currents, like the Gulf Stream, make great paths in the sea. Nansen also used his instruments to record water temperature and the force and direction of winds.

The *Viking* sailed to Spitzbergen, a group of remote islands east of Greenland.

At that time they were inhabited only in summer, when fishing and sealing ships anchored offshore. The baby seals, which the *Viking* hunted, were born here on the beaches. Their fur and fat were valuable.

The islands were snowy even in summer, and giant ice cakes, called ice floes, floated in the sea. Fridtjof loved the strange cold silence of this arctic land, and the beauty of the Northern Lights. He kept a journal and made many sketches.

Since Nansen was such a good shot, the captain put him in charge of one of the seal boats. The *Viking* caught many seals, as they sunned themselves on the beaches and ice floes.

Suddenly it grew very cold, and the channels between the ice floes began to freeze. The ship became trapped in the ice. The flow of the current carried the ice, and the *Viking*, westward to the east coast of Greenland.

Nansen gazed in wonder at the huge, icy cliffs that rose almost straight from the sea. Beyond these mountains was a cap of ice and snow that covered most of Greenland.

"I would like to go ashore and explore," said Nansen, but the captain forbade it.

"The ice might carry the ship away before we could pick you up again," he said. "No one lives on this coast. Greenland's settlements are all on the warmer west coast."

Nansen was disappointed, but he was kept busy hunting, as the *Viking* needed fresh meat. Many polar bears appeared on the ice around the ship. The lookout in the crow's nest would shout, "Polar bear! Polar bear!" Nansen would leap

from the ship to the ice with his rifle
and a knife, wearing gym shoes and no
coat so he could run faster. He seldom
failed to kill a bear. His last hunt was
his most adventurous.

The polar bear had seen Nansen and
started to run away. When it came to a
gap in the ice sheet it plunged into the

water. Nansen tried to jump over the gap but he fell in too. He tossed his gun onto the ice, but it slid into the water and he had to dive for it. Nansen found his gun, scrambled out of the water, and shot the bear in the back. Roaring with anger, the bear started to climb onto the ice to attack Nansen.

Nansen fired again and this time killed the great beast. It began to slip down into the water. Nansen grabbed it by its ears and stood there dripping wet in below zero temperature.

He shouted to the men on shipboard. The captain and several men came running to help him. "Return to the ship and put on dry clothes," the captain ordered Nansen.

On his way back to the ship, Nansen saw another bear, and chased after it. When the bear came to open water, it swam. So did Nansen. The bear climbed up on the ice again. So did Nansen. He was nearly five miles from the ship before he got close enough to shoot the bear.

Nansen was calmly skinning it with his knife when one of the crew came to help him carry it to the ship.

Nansen was a puzzle to the tough seamen. When it was bitter cold he appeared to be even tougher than they were. He was not afraid of anything.

He wrestled with them and he sang songs and told stories. They accepted him as one of them.

However, the men could not understand his scientific experiments. Why did he examine samples of sea water with his microscope? Why did he study the insides of seals and birds? To them, it seemed a waste of time.

As the *Viking* drifted, frozen fast in the ice floe, Nansen was surprised to find dust, slime, and dirt on the ice. He collected samples. When he saw a log embedded in the ice, he cut off a piece to add to his collection. He tried to tell the crew why this was important.

"Spitzbergen and nearby Greenland, have no trees," he said. "They have only willow and birch shrubs. I want to find out where this wood and dirt come from. Perhaps these ice floes have floated all the way from Siberia, far to the northeast. Some day I want to chart the currents that brought them here."

4

Greenland Beckons

When Nansen returned from the sealing expedition, he was asked to become curator of a museum at Bergen, Norway. It was a flattering offer for a young man.

"I think you should accept this offer," Professor Collett told him. "The Bergen Museum has a fine reputation. Now that zoology is your chosen field, you can continue your research there."

During more than five years at the museum, Nansen wrote many scientific articles on the nervous systems of sea creatures. He worked towards his doctorate in zoology, and he also held classes in nature study for boys and girls.

Whenever he could get away, he went on skiing or walking trips with his dog and gun. Such trips followed the pattern of his youth—he carried little food and slept on the bare ground.

During these years the great glittering ice cap of Greenland beckoned to him. Nansen wanted to cross it but no one had ever succeeded. Could it be done on skis? Among the several men who had tried and failed was the famous Swedish explorer, Nils Nordenskiöld. Nansen went to Sweden to talk with him.

Nordenskiöld was familiar with Nansen's growing reputation as a scientist and his renown as a champion skier. But when

Nansen explained his bold plan to cross Greenland from east to west, Nordenskiöld shook his head. All previous expeditions had started from villages on the west coast.

"Start from the east coast, young man? No! It's too dangerous! If you were to fail and had to turn back, there would be no people to provide food and shelter. Your own ship could not wait for you, for it might get crushed in the ice floes."

"If we can't retreat we shall be forced to go forward," said Nansen calmly. "Remember, all the expeditions that started from the west coast had to carry extra food and supplies for their return journey. If I make only the one journey, east to west, I can depend on finding food at my destination. Light loads make faster travel."

Nordenskiöld was finally convinced. But the Norwegian government refused to give Nansen money for such a dangerous expedition. However, Greenland belonged to Denmark, and a leading Danish citizen offered the necessary funds.

During the next winter Nansen studied hard for his graduate school examinations. He also ordered equipment for the planned expedition. Included were special sledges, skis, snowshoes, boots, clothes, and sleeping bags. He ordered a new kind of pemmican—chopped dried meat mixed with raisins—chocolate, condensed milk, biscuits, cheese, and other kinds of food used by explorers. He tested everything himself.

Nansen advertised for five men to go on the trip. From the 40 that applied, he made his choice. Otto Sverdrup, a Norwegian sea captain, was very steady and reliable. The two other Norwegians picked were fine skiers. Nansen also chose two Lapps from Finland who had spent their lives on skis herding reindeer.

The expedition went to Iceland to board a sealing ship, the *Jason*. On June 11, 1888, the *Jason* reached Cape Dan, half-way down the east coast of Greenland. Nansen had arranged to have the ship leave the expedition here, but ten miles of grinding ice floes lay between ship and shore. So the ship sailed on, farther south, looking for a place to land the expedition.

At last the channel widened to open water. It was then that Nansen decided to land, so he had two rowboats lowered. Two Norwegians and one Lapp crowded into each boat, along with the supplies. The men waved good-bye to the crew, and the sealing ship went on its way.

Soon trouble started. Ice floes began to close in on the small boats. One boat was hit by a sharp piece of ice.

"We are leaking badly," Nansen said. "We must land on this ice floe to make repairs."

The men hauled both boats up on the

ice island. By the time they had repaired the boat, the water around them had completely frozen over. So they set up a tent where the six men would sleep. They could not cook and had to eat cold food.

The current carried the ice floe far to the south. Huge ice floes thundered and

crashed around them, and water swept through their tent. The men sang songs and told stories, to keep up their spirits.

Ten long days passed while the men drifted southward. They could no longer see Greenland's coastline. Then, by luck, the current changed, and it began to bear their ice island shoreward again. They were 300 miles farther south than Nansen had hoped to land, so when they reached open water they launched their boats and rowed back northward.

After twelve days, they landed on a narrow beach beneath towering ice cliffs. To celebrate, they had a fine meal of hot chocolate, oat cakes, and cranberry jam.

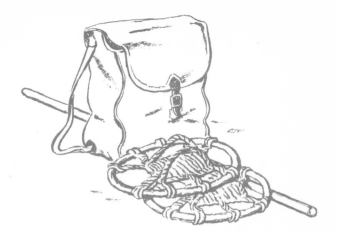

5

Across the Ice Cap

In August, two months after the men had left the *Jason*, they began the tough climb up the steep, ice-coated mountain. Four of the men drew a sledge each. Nansen and Sverdrup together pulled the fifth sledge, which was twice as heavy as the others.

The men wore snowshoes which helped them to grip the ice. Each carried a pole

to plunge into the snow in search of crevasses. A man might fall into one of these great snow-covered cracks in the ice and plunge to his death. That first day the men traveled only a few miles.

The third day it began to rain, and for the next three days they lived in their tent. This further delay worried Nansen, for supplies were running low and food had to be rationed. From then on the men were never free from hunger.

When the rains stopped, they forged ahead again and came upon the great rounded ice cap that covered the interior of Greenland. It stretched ahead like an endless white desert. Each day Nansen recorded the weather and the depth of the snow. He believed that the ice sheet was at least 1000 feet thick.

The hot midday sun melted the snow's

surface, making the sledges hard to pull. The sledge straps cut cruelly into the men's shoulders, and the bitter wind blew constantly against them. The nights were extremely cold.

Although they hardly noticed the slope, the men were going uphill. Nansen was headed for a village called Christianshaab in northwest Greenland. His men were worn out from struggling against the terrible wind, and winter was rapidly approaching.

"We had better change our plans and head for Godthaab instead," he said to Sverdrup. "It is nearer."

Sverdrup agreed. "It is farther south and the change in direction will put the wind behind us. We could even put sails on the sledges."

By September 14th the expedition had

reached the peak of the ice caps. They had come 150 miles; 200 miles more lay ahead. The sledges were lighter, for they had less food to carry. They could even race the sledges now, as they were going downhill.

Three days later Sverdrup shouted, "Land ahead!" Far away stretched a dark coastline free of snow.

Farther on, the snow ended and rocks and rough earth were visible. The sledges were now useless, so the men made packs of the remaining supplies for their backs. Suddenly they came upon rough grass and heather and the air smelled of juniper bushes. It was a wonderful change after a month of snow and ice. The men threw themselves down in the heather, sniffed it, and rolled in it. Here, too, was willow scrub to burn and water to cook with.

Nansen knew that the tiny village of Godthaab (Good Hope) lay farther south. But the cliffs between them and the village were steep and dangerous. "We are close to a fjord," Nansen told Sverdrup. "I think that two of us should go ahead by sea and send back a rescue party for the others." Sverdrup agreed.

They built a canoe frame of willow branches and tent poles and covered it with tent canvas. It would carry only two men, Nansen and Sverdrup. They were risking their lives if they should meet a sudden storm.

Fortunately the weather remained good. Hour after hour the men paddled with their canvas-covered willow paddles. When they reached Godthaab the excited villagers greeted them with a salute of guns. A heavy storm broke, but as soon as it

cleared, Nansen sent back a rescue party to pick up the other men.

No ships came in winter to this ice-bound harbor, and the last ship of the season had gone. Nansen sent off a swift one-man kayak, with letters, to overtake the last ship, so that people in Norway would know that the expedition was a success.

The Danes in Godthaab were friendly, but Nansen chose to live in a nearby Eskimo settlement until spring. There he could study Eskimo customs and learn their language. He was especially interested in the wood used by the Eskimos. He wanted to know where it came from.

On his return from the sealing expedition seven years before, he had sent the mud and driftwood he had collected to other scientists. They claimed it had come from Siberia. If this driftwood came from Siberia too, it would help to prove his theory about the arctic current. He felt sure that the current moved north over the Polar region, then south once more between Spitzbergen and Greenland. A branch of the current must then flow around Greenland and up this west coast.

On May 30th the expedition returned to Christiania by ship. Cheering crowds welcomed them. Almost everyone had said it was impossible to cross Greenland, but Nansen and his five companions had done it. They were heroes to all of Norway.

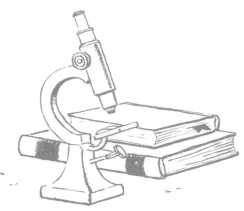

6

Forward the *Fram*

It was natural that Nansen should meet his future wife while skiing. He saw her skis, then her boots, sticking out of a snowdrift. He picked her up and brushed her off. Laughing, they exchanged names. The pretty, dark-haired young woman was Eva Sars. She was the daughter of Michael Sars, a professor of zoology at the University of Christiania. She was a musician and a fine singer.

When they became engaged, Fridtjof warned Eva, "I am going to the North Pole some day."

"Good!" she said. "I will go with you."

For a time the couple lived in an apartment in Christiania, but they both missed the country. Soon they built a house a little way out of town. Nansen was working at the university now, and he was also writing two long books. One of these was called *Eskimo Life*.

Next Nansen wanted to explore the Polar Region. For years, explorers had tried to reach the North Pole, but all had failed. Some had died in the attempt. No one knew for sure if there was land at the North Pole, or simply ice. Nansen believed that the free flow of the drift ice made the existence of land unlikely.

The fearful cold, wind, and fog in the

Arctic, with the long winter darkness made travel there dangerous and difficult. Previously men had tried to cross the rough drift ice on foot. Nansen believed there was a new and safe way to reach the Polar region.

The driftwood from Greenland had indeed proved to be of Siberian origin. Nansen was sure now that his theory about the arctic current was correct. If he could take a ship north of Siberia and let it freeze into the ice, the ship and ice would be carried farther north by the current. Then they would be swept across the Arctic Ocean and south again to open water near Greenland.

"Our trip may take several years," he told Eva. "But we will be warm and comfortable in the ship. If the ship drifts close to the Pole, we might even cross it."

Even more important to Nansen than reaching the Pole, was the charting of the arctic current. Large numbers of fish are found in cold currents. Norway's main support was its fishing industry. Greater knowledge of ocean currents would be of enormous value to Norway.

For such a voyage Nansen designed a special ship. He talked over his plans with Eva.

"The ship will be short and chunky," he explained, "like a wooden shoe. If her sides are rounded she won't be crushed by the ice floes, as other ships have been in the Arctic. Instead she will be squeezed up and out of the ice."

Nansen's expedition across Greenland had made him famous. The Norwegian government now agreed to finance the new expedition.

Nansen took his ship design to Colin Archer, a Scottish shipbuilder with ship-yards in Christiania. "The ship must be very strong," he said. "It must withstand the pressure of ice around it. We will need several layers of oak and pine." For warmth they would line the ship with cork and linoleum.

Nansen's carefully chosen crew of twelve included engineers, a doctor, scientists,

and seamen. All were excellent skiers and willing to work at any task. "It will probably be a three year voyage," Nansen warned them, "but we will take supplies for six years." Otto Sverdrup would be the captain.

"This time we will take sledge dogs," Nansen told Sverdrup. "If we have to abandon the ship, the dogs will pull the supply sledges."

In October, 1891, Eva Nansen christened the new vessel *Fram* (Forward). But Eva could not go on the trip since the Nansens now had a little daughter, Liv. Eva saw the *Fram* off from Christiania in June. The new expedition sailed up the coast and left Vardö, the last Norwegian port, on July 21, 1893.

7

Drifting with the Ice

The *Fram* traveled northeast toward the Arctic Circle. Khabarovo, in Russian Siberia, was her last port of call. Here she took on 34 Russian sledge dogs, which Nansen had ordered. They were housed in kennels on the foredeck, where they howled and barked all night.

At Khabarovo everyone sent letters home. This would be their last chance to communicate for some years, for in those days a ship had no radio.

North of Siberia, Nansen charted and

named many small barren islands. Some of the men went ashore to gather specimens of rocks and plants. Others hunted deer, bear, seals, and walrus.

It grew very cold and daylight hours were short. By September 20th the *Fram* had reached the edge of the ice pack. The ice began to close in around them.

The ship's specially designed propeller was removed so the ice would not damage it. The ice soon froze completely around the ship. Now the *Fram* would drift with the ice wherever the current carried it.

On October 26th the sun sank, not to rise again for four months. The *Fram* manufactured her own electricity, and she had a large library and well-equipped workshops. Nansen planned to keep the men busy making any new equipment they might need. He knew that idleness during the dark winter months could make them homesick and quarrelsome.

Day and night, Nansen conducted his scientific observations. He chopped through the ice and measured the temperature of the water beneath, he measured its saltiness, and the thickness of the ice. The ocean proved surprisingly deep. Nansen examined samples of mud and sea life under the microscope. He also recorded the winds.

Nansen's chief interest was in the ocean currents and how far the ice drifted with the current. Every day he and his crew calculated the *Fram's* position by the position of the stars. The only man to complain of not enough work was the doctor, for the men were so healthy. Finally he took charge of the dogs.

On October 9th the *Fram* faced her

first real test. During the afternoon there was a deafening crash. Everyone rushed out on deck. The *Fram* was forced up as much as two feet by the pressure of the ice around her. For two days the ice floes creaked and groaned against her sides. But they could not crush her stout timbers. She merely slid up and out of their grasp, as Nansen had planned. The next time the *Fram* was squeezed no one worried. They knew she was safe.

Nansen planned plenty of amusement to break the monotony. Each man's birthday was an excuse for a party—with candles, a cake, and singing. They celebrated the Norwegian holidays. Christmas was the best of all, for everyone had made small presents for each other. They sang and played musical instruments.

When spring came the men trained the

dogs with the sledges on the ice. They hunted bear and walrus for food and kept in good physical condition with games and running. Soon the brief arctic summer was ended and another long winter began.

The drift of the current was carrying the *Fram* northward but not as close to to Pole as Nansen had hoped. One day he called Sverdrup into his cabin. "If we are to reach the Pole," he said, "I think we must plan to travel on foot. We can start in March, as soon as daylight returns."

"I will take one man with me," he went on. "I wish it could be you. But we can't both leave the *Fram*. You are the only one with enough experience to be left in charge."

Sverdrup was disappointed, but he understood. "We will each go forward in our own way. *Fram!*"

8

Towards the North Pole

All that long winter the *Fram's* work-shops were busy making equipment for Nansen. He needed two sledges, two strong kayaks, and skis. Dogs would pull the sledges. When the men reached open water, they would travel by kayak.

Nansen's plans did not include a return to the *Fram*. It would be difficult to find where it had drifted. After exploring the

North Pole, Nansen would head for either Franz Josef Land or Spitzbergen, where the sealing and fishing ships came.

Nansen arranged for any emergency on the *Fram*. "The ship should near Greenland the summer after next," he told Sverdrup, "and break free of the ice. We will meet in Norway that August."

Nansen chose Hjalmar Johansen as his companion. Johansen was a fine athlete and an expert skier. In midwinter the two men moved from the ship to live on the ice. There they tested the new equipment and trained the sledge dogs. On March 14th, 1895, they waved good-bye to the *Fram* and her crew. Would they really ever meet again?

At first the ice was smooth and the dog sledges made good headway. The sun, just returned, was up only a short time each day. But they traveled by moonlight and the Northern Lights. Then they reached great piles of rough ice, often 30 feet high, that had been thrown up by crashing ice floes.

The men had to lift the sledges, and sometimes even the dogs, over the ice piles. The men were so weary that they dozed on their skis and even slept and fell down. In camp, Nansen fed the dogs, and Johansen made a meal of hot pemmican and soup. Then they crawled into their sleeping bags to get warm while they ate.

Sometimes they came to open channels of water. Here the sledges had to be unloaded and everything, including the dogs, put in the kayaks to cross to the farther bank. The men continued to ski and walk, day after day, day after day.

They struggled constantly against the bitter arctic wind. The wind and ice were far worse than Nansen had expected. The country in all directions was unchanging ice with no land in sight.

In April they discovered that the great sheet of ice was drifting south faster than they were moving north.

"We have reached farther north than anyone has come before," Nansen told Johansen. "Our supplies are getting low. We must turn back."

They set two Norwegian flags into the ice sheet at latitude 86° 13.6′ North. Though they had been unable to reach the Pole, they had made an important discovery. They had proved that no land continent surrounded the Pole. The water could not be so deep, nor the ice drifting so fast, if there were land nearby.

9

The Longest Winter

Nansen and Johansen headed for Franz Josef Land, 400 miles to the south.

The men's watches were an extremely important part of their scientific equipment. Each day, exactly at noon, Nansen measured the angle of the sun to the earth. This told him how far east or west they had traveled.

One morning when he woke, Nansen glanced at his watch. It had stopped.

"What time is it?" he asked Johansen. But the night before Johansen had also been too weary to wind his watch.

Nansen set his watch by guess, but he could no longer reckon their exact position. By the last of April they had reached the place where Franz Josef Land should have been. But they were still on the ice, with no land in sight.

May was warmer and the days were longer, but the melting snow made the sledges harder to pull. Supplies were dangerously low, and there were no bears or walrus to kill. One by one the dogs died of exhaustion and starvation. Finally only three dogs were left. Nansen and Johansen had to help pull the sledges, so some days they traveled only a mile.

On June 22nd they killed two seals and feasted on raw meat and blubber. They even made delicious pancakes of seal blood and some of the remaining flour. But Nansen was worried. The arctic summer was very short. What would happen if they were still on this ice when winter came again?

Finally a month later they saw a white coastline in the distance. "It has long haunted our dreams, this land," Nansen wrote in his journal, "and now it comes like a vision."

It took them two weeks, however, to reach open water. They then made good speed sailing in the two kayaks, tied together. They passed a string of barren islands. Were these part of Franz Josef Land? They could not be sure.

Some evenings they camped on shore.

There were walrus and seal to shoot and plenty to eat. But the days were getting very short, and they could see new ice ahead.

Finally on August 24th Nansen made his decision. "We shall have to spend the winter here on one of the islands. We can build a hut of stones to live in and shoot game to eat."

They dug a foundation with a walrus bone. Then they lugged stones to build a twelve feet by six feet hut and packed moss between the stones. The rafters of driftwood held up a low roof of walrus hide. Their entrance was a tunnel like those the Eskimos build, curtained with bearskin to keep out the cold.

This was their home all that long winter. It was dark and bitterly cold, but they had frozen enough meat to keep

from starving. The blubber, which they
burned in the tiny fireplace, covered the
men with grease. There was no way for
them to wash it off.

Sometimes Nansen and Johansen crawled
out for a short walk. Their clothes had
become so tattered they did not keep out
the cold. They slept much of the time,
but it was a long wait for the sun to

appear again. The two men never quarreled nor grew to hate each other, as so many other arctic explorers had done.

On May 19th, 1896, Nansen and his companion set out again to find their way to Norway. At first they traveled on skis, pulling the sledges over the ice, since there were now no dogs. Later they reached open water and could sail in the kayaks.

The kayaks were crowded and uncomfortable. One day after they had landed to stretch their legs, Johansen glanced back.

"The kayaks are loose!" he shouted.

"Here, take my watch!" Nansen cried. Then he leaped into the water to catch the boats. The wind had caught the sails, and the kayaks were drifting fast. Nansen remembered that everything they owned was aboard them. He did not have a knife or a gun. Desperately he forced his frozen limbs to keep moving.

When he finally reached the boats, he was so chilled and exhausted he could hardly climb aboard. Yet, when he saw two large birds, he recalled how short of food he and Johansen were and shot them.

When he landed, Johansen pulled off Nansen's frozen clothes and wrapped him in a sleeping bag and the tent. Johansen

brought him back to life with hot soup made from the two birds.

On the morning of June 17th, they were exploring on shore. Suddenly Nansen heard a dog bark. Soon he saw dog tracks in the snow. He climbed an ice hummock to look around and heard a voice shout to the dog. He ran down toward the voice.

He saw a man, clean and well dressed, walking with a gun and a dog. The man came toward him. "I am so glad to see you," he said in English. "Have you a ship here?"

Tattered and filthy, Nansen held out his hand. "I have no ship. I have only one companion."

Suddenly the man recognized him. "You must be Nansen! I have been hoping to find you. I am Frederick Jackson."

Jackson, an Englishman, had for two

years been exploring Franz Josef Land.
His ship, the *Windward*, would call for
him here in a month.

The happy Norwegians moved into
Jackson's comfortable camp to wait for
the ship. What a thrill it was to sleep
in a warm bed, to wash, and to have
plenty of food! Best of all were the letters
from home which Jackson had with him.
He had hoped that the *Fram* might stop
here, in Franz Josef Land.

10
Joyous Return

Six weeks later Nansen and Johansen left on the *Windward*, homeward bound. Then on the evening of August 12th the dark line of Norway's hills appeared against the sky. Lieutenant Johansen, an expert gymnast, celebrated by walking around the deck on his hands. Both he and Nansen were too excited to sleep. Next morning the *Windward* dropped anchor in Vardö harbor, from which the *Fram* sailed over three years before.

Nansen hurried ashore and handed a

package of telegrams to the telegraph office. These were to the Norwegian government, newspapers, scientific societies, and sponsors of the voyage. The manager read the first telegram, which was to Eva. He came to the signature.

"You're Nansen himself! Impossible!" and he nearly wept with joy.

Suddenly the news spread throughout Vardö. Norwegian flags began to flutter from every window. Enthusiastic crowds followed the two explorers through the streets.

Sir George Baden-Powell, an English friend of Nansen's, had been cruising on his yacht, the *Otaria*. He was anchored at nearby Hammerfest. Baden-Powell insisted that the explorers come aboard as his guests. Soon Eva and four-year-old Liv joined them. Joy was added to joy.

Only one thing was needed. Where was the *Fram*? Nansen had expected the ship to break free of the ice that August.

Early on the morning of August 20th, Baden-Powell brought the manager of the telegraph office to Nansen's cabin. He had a telegram which read, "Skjaervo, Aug. 20, 1896. 9:00 a.m. *Fram* arrived here today in good condition. All well on board. Leaving at once for Tromsö.

Welcome home." It was signed "Otto Sverdrup."

Up came the *Otaria's* anchor. She had barely dropped anchor again at Tromsö, a seaport south of Vardö, when the *Fram's* crew crowded aboard. Grinning broadly, they pounded Nansen on the back and shook Johansen's hand.

Everything had gone just as Nansen had planned it, including the day that he thought the *Fram* would reach open water. Nansen was already famous for his amazing trek across the Polar ice. Now his skill as an organizer won him new acclaim. Newspapers all over the world carried word of his accomplishments.

As the *Otaria* and the *Fram* steamed south, boats of all kinds put out from every fjord and some joined the joyful journey to Christiania. Every headland was crowded with gay flags and people waving and cheering, to welcome home Norway's heroes. When the fleet moved into Christiania fjord, Nansen steered toward Colin Archer's shipyard where the *Fram* had been built. There, warships, torpedo boats, 130 steamers and countless small craft came to pay tribute to the *Fram*, the stoutest warrior of them all.

After four days of banquets and

speeches in Christiania, Nansen began to get restless. He told Sverdrup, "I wish I were back in the the silence and solitude of the Arctic!"

Soon he settled down with his family outside the city. He was now a full professor at the university and he was busy writing about his scientific findings in the Arctic. One book (dedicated to Eva Nansen), *Farthest North*, was the story of the *Fram* and the dash for the Pole. It was very popular with boys and girls, as well as grownups.

As the years went by, the Nansen family grew. Their house became too small for the two girls and three boys. Nansen took Eva to see a site he had chosen for a new house, "Polhögda"—Polarheight. It was a high cliff looking out over a fjord.

"Every room will have a view of the

sea," he told her. "We will have space for all my books and my instruments."

Nansen had now decided what his life's work would be—the study of the oceans of the world. Oceanography was a new subject and he could help answer some of the world's questions. How deep down was the bottom of the sea? How fast do ocean currents move, and in what directions? How cold or warm are the ocean currents? What fish could be found in previously unexplored parts of the ocean? Where were the most fish?

All these things were of special concern to Norway. Her main export was dried fish, especially cod and herring. It was generally believed that such fish could be found only in shallow coastal waters. Nansen was almost certain that this theory was wrong. Ships had reported seeing these fish far out at sea.

Nansen was put in charge of a ship especially equipped for scientific research at sea. This was the *Michael Sars*, named for Eva's father, the famous marine zoologist. It set out in midsummer of 1900 with a group of dedicated researchers. Nansen and the scientists would cruise between Greenland and Iceland.

One day on the way to Iceland, Nansen watched anxiously as the first net was hauled in from the deep water. It was filled with bright glittering herring and a few codfish.

"So I was right!" Nansen exclaimed. "Such fish can be caught far out at sea."

This discovery would greatly widen the fishing grounds of Norway and even of Iceland. Nansen had made another contribution to his beloved country.

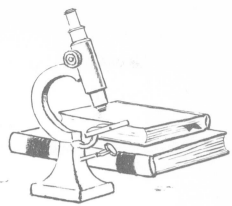

11
The South Pole

Nansen was teaching oceanography at the university, lecturing in both Europe and America, and continuing to write. But he found time to help Otto Sverdrup plan an expedition to the ice field west of Greenland. He loaned Sverdrup the *Fram*. Sverdrup charted some thousands of miles of land and sea ice that had not been explored before.

Nansen, himself, had further plans for the stout little ship. He wanted to take her to the Antarctic and explore around the South Pole. One day a young Norwegian explorer named Roald Amundsen came to see him. Amundsen was the first man to have taken a ship through the Northwest Passage, the waterway north of Canada.

Amundsen had come to ask Nansen if he might buy the *Fram*. "I want to try to find the North Pole," he said.

Nansen hesitated a bit. Then he told Amundsen of his own plan. "Why not go with me to Antarctica?" he said.

At this time, Nansen was too busy to make such a voyage. For years Norway had been ruled by Sweden but in 1905 she gained her independence. She called on Nansen to be her first ambassador to England. He hesitated for some time but finally accepted.

A year after their first talk Amundsen returned to see Nansen. On his way down from his tower study, Nansen found Eva in the library.

"Amundsen is here," he told her.

Eva turned white. "I know what you plan to do," she said sadly. "You will go with him and be gone for years, as you were before."

Nansen said nothing. He went to join the younger explorer. "You may have the *Fram*," he said. "I have decided not to make my trip."

Several months later, Nansen was in England. He received word that Eva had become suddenly ill. She died before he could reach home. Nansen was now free to explore, but he felt it would be unfair to ask Amundsen to return the *Fram*.

In 1910 the *Fram* sailed away from

Christiania. Roald Amundsen was on the bridge. Since Robert E. Peary had discovered the North Pole the year before, Amundsen was now on his way to the Antarctic.

This was one of the saddest hours of Nansen's life. He had lost both his wife and his ship. But Nansen rejoiced with Norway when Amundsen became the first man ever to reach the South Pole.

12

Nansen Belongs to the World

When Nansen became Norway's ambassador to England at the age of 45, he discovered a new career. For the next 25 years, he had little time for science and none for exploration. He was now a statesman.

During World War I, Nansen was sent to the United States to obtain food for the starving people of neutral Norway. Nansen was saddened by the terrible war. When it was over, an organization to keep peace in the world was formed. It was called the League of Nations. Nansen worked to make sure the small, neutral Scandinavian countries were included in the League.

"The League is the great hope of world peace," he said.

One of the League's first tasks was to bring home all of the prisoners of war scattered throughout Europe and Asia. More than half of these men were in prison camps in Russia, where revolutionists had overthrown the Czar and started the Soviet form of government.

Nansen was asked to head the committee which was to arrange for the prisoners' return. His job was extremely difficult, as the countries of Europe were very poor after the long war. This made it hard to get money to buy food, clothing, and medicine for the prisoners. It was harder still to get transportation to take the prisoners home.

Nansen worked patiently to solve these problems. He gave speeches everywhere and raised enough money to provide immediate care for the prisoners. He spoke to the heads of many governments. The Soviet government agreed to provide trains to move prisoners as far as the Russian frontiers. The English loaned ships, and the Germans loaned sailors to take prisoners home. In eighteen months, over 400,000 men were set free.

Later Nansen's committee helped the Russian refugees to find homes and jobs in other countries. These men had fought against the new Soviet government and had fled from their homeland.

People who were still in Russia were dying of hunger because of a terrible

famine. Nansen worked hard to raise money for food and clothing. People in America also gave money.

The problems of the homeless and hungry continued to concern Nansen. In the early 1920's, there was a war between Greece and Turkey. Many Greeks were driven from their homes by the conquering Turks. The Greek government had no money with which to help their refugees. Nansen went to Greece, settled the refugees in tent cities, and found them unused land where new farms and villages could be built. He got the League of Nations to lend Greece money to pay for their resettlement.

During those years, Nansen received many honors, including the Nobel Peace Prize. Later he became the Norwegian delegate to the League of Nations.

But still his greatest joy was to escape to the forests and mountains of Norway. In January 1930, he went skiing with some friends. Nansen was 69 now and tired from his years of hard work. He dropped behind his friends. Someone returned and found Nansen leaning on his long ski pole, gazing out over the hills.

Nansen said, a little sadly, "I always used to lead the party. Now I cannot even follow."

The following spring as he sat on his porch, his son's wife noticed that his head had dropped on his chest. He had not gone to sleep. He had died peacefully, looking out at the blue waters of the northern sea that he loved so much.

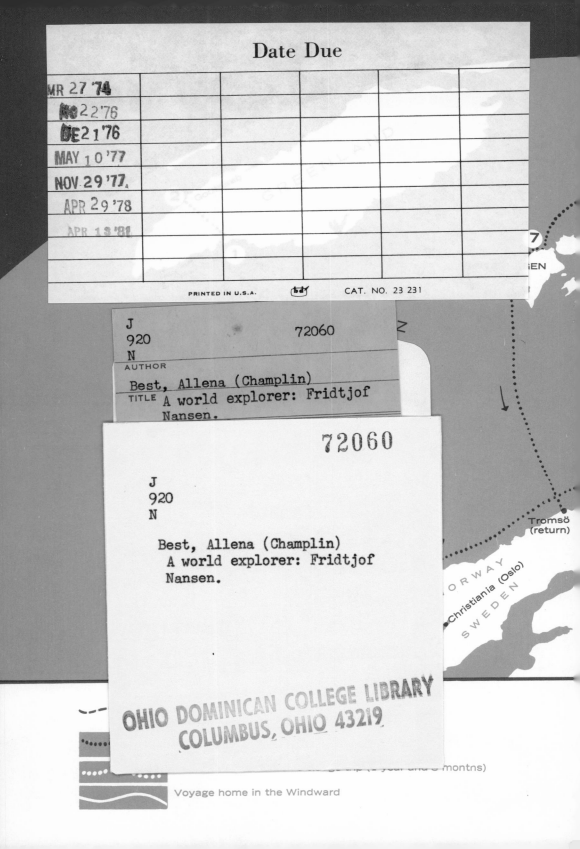

Voyage home in the Windward